WALK THE TALK:

LIVING A LIFE OF FAITH IN ACTION

WALK THE TALK

Living a Life of Faith in Action

RUNETTIA U. GUESS

FOREWORD BY
DR. ZELPHINE SMITH-DIXON

PALMETTO
P U B L I S H I N G
Charleston, SC
www.PalmettoPublishing.com

Copyright © 2024 by Runettia U. Guess

All rights reserved

No portion of this book may be reproduced, stored in a retrieval system, or transmitted in any form by any means–electronic, mechanical, photocopy, recording, or other–except for brief quotations in printed reviews, without prior permission of the author.

Paperback ISBN: 979-8-8229-5011-5
eBook ISBN: 979-8-8229-5012-2

Flourish Visions

To my daughter Jessica, you are and have always been my rock. Thank you for your confidence in me and for never letting me lose sight of what God has called me to do. I love you to life.

To each of you, I hope that as you immerse yourself in this daily devotional that you are inspired to seek a deeper relationship with God. My prayer is that your trust deepens, and you grow in meekness along your faith journey.

FOREWORD

As I drove down the highway, I had a spirit of expectation that the Holy Spirit would speak to my heart and deepen my revelation concerning living a life of faith in action. By no means am I a poster child for faith, but my lived experiences created a catalyst by which living without faith wasn't an option. I immediately considered that faith is a verb and requires ACTION! I couldn't explain why so many believers stop believing. I don't mean stop believing in God but stop believing in the abundance of who He is. Simply putting faith in action is insufficient without putting a demand on the posture of courage, consistency, and clarity.

The nature of banking allows you to link an account that provides overdraft protection if you ever become overdrawn. Faith puts a demand on the supernatural so you don't deplete your natural self. This is not the season of depletion but one of duplication! Faith not only produces results but reproduces life.

Courage gives you permission to get started. Have you ever attempted to move a car with the emergency brakes on? This is the equivelant of living a life without faith. Often we assume that having courage means no fear! Actually, it is the exact opposite. Fear is a natural response, and courage is a supernatural response. I choose courage because I can't do it alone.

Deuteronomy 31:6 teaches us to "Be strong and courageous. Do not be afraid or terrified because of them, for the Lord your God goes with you; he will never leave you nor forsake you."

Living a life of fear implies I can only do what I trust myself to accomplish. Living a life of faith implies I can do all things that I trust God to accomplish.

About this time, I heard the Holy Spirit direct me to look over. I glanced off the interstate and saw a beautiful rainbow to my left. It quickened my spirit and reminded me that the promises of God are yes and amen. Trusting God's plan when you can't trace His hand takes courage, and courage produces faith. Faith produces character. As I researched the rainbow, I was baffled to learn that there's more to a rainbow than what meets the earthly eye. A rainbow is more than an arch but a full circle that isn't always visible. Why? That's a great question! It takes a much more elevated perspective to see the fullness of His promise. What if I told you it's coming full circle?

Consistency reminds us that faith is more than action—it's a lifestyle, and daily practice is required! You have to choose to make faith your choice of habit. Consistency is necessary for branding and marketing! God wants to display His glory using your story. Hurt, shame, disappointment, frustration, pain, trauma, drama, and grief—God can use all of it.

Consistency does not mean perfection but being reliably and reasonably perfected. Small steps matter. We have the DNA of our father, and He is faithful.

I'm reminded of the Our Father Prayer—Give us this day our daily bread! A faith-based lifestyle feels less like a sprint and more like a marathon. The race isn't given to the swift but to the one who holds out to the end.

How do you walk the talk when every day isn't equal? Stand on His word and pray for clarity! Courage gets you started. Consistency gives you work ethic to practice and pray. Clarity grants purpose and meaning to a life well lived. One of my favorite scriptures is that "all things work together for the good of them who love the Lord and are called according to his purpose" (Romans 8:28). Whenever I find myself at a crossroad called crisis, I look to the cross to bring clarity to my call. He's got to make it work together for good. Everything you're called to costs you!

I am so honored to write this foreword and believe this devotional, grounded in biblical teachings from James, will be a blessing. The author is no stranger to being tried by fire but does not smell like smoke. Her story is one of faith and resilience! I absolutely love her glimpses of transparency for the sake of transformation. Transformation is possible, but it does take community! More importantly, it takes faith! Will you commit to walk the talk?

— Dr. Zelphine Smith-Dixon

Day 1

Faith Keeps Us

Dear brothers and sisters, when troubles of any kind come your way, consider it an opportunity for great joy. For you know that when your faith is tested, your endurance has a chance to grow. So let it grow, for when your endurance is fully developed, you will be perfect and complete, needing nothing. — James 1:2–4 (NLT)

As our son lay in a hospital bed connected to a ventilator, I questioned whether God was good. It was hard for me to think about His goodness. When my sisters spoke of God working in their lives and showing Himself to be faithful to them, I had to fight back the tears. Most of the time, I had to leave the room. *Really, God? You're good now? Because I don't feel that way.*

> **God uses every situation to grow our faith.**

For many of us, our struggles may raise similar questions. We begin to question whether God is in control as we struggle to feel His presence amid our internal chaos. Or maybe our emotions cause us to remain focused on our circumstances and not on who God is. God does not ask that we ignore our pain but rather that we look to Him in our trials and tests. Sometimes this may be hard to do. We must remember that our suffering is never pointless, for God can make everything work together for the good of those who love Him (Romans 8:28). This is His promise to us. that He will use every trial to bring about something meaningful in our lives, if we trust Him. With each test, we have an opportunity to grow our faith as we deepen our trust in God.

As Christians we are equipped to find joy in our suffering through prayer and by drawing closer to God. We must ask God for wisdom to be gained from our trials and seek to use every situation to grow our faith deeper and stronger. Even as Christ was crucified, He remained faithful (Hebrews 12:2). His obedience was rewarded with His seat at the right hand of the throne of God. The same God who fulfilled that promise has promised those of us who remain faithful to Him that we will receive the crown of life. This means that through difficulties and uncertainties we can trust Him to make each of our tests of faith a link in a chain of good things to come. We must look for the good in our trials and trust God to remain steadfast in His promise to us.

Father, we know that You are with us even during our difficult times. We are aware that there is a purpose in all we experience. We acknowledge that, as we ask, You will provide us with wisdom to stay steadfast in our commitment to you. We petition You to help us increase the endurance of our faith so we may reap the crown of life. In Jesus's name, Amen.

Day 2

Call to Action

Understand this, my dear brothers and sisters: You must all be quick to listen, slow to speak, and slow to get angry. Human anger does not produce the righteousness God desires.
— James 1:19–20 (NLT)

There was a time when I was quick to vocalize my thoughts. I rejected a lot of what others had to say to me. I was easily irritated and quickly became frustrated and angry. I can recall that time of my life to be mentally, emotionally, and spiritually exhausting. I'm sure my exhaustion was largely the result of my ungodly behavior toward others and even myself. There were plenty of times when I asked for forgiveness for my behavior. We all can relate to having feelings of anger and times when we have rejected others or responded in an ungodly way. Maybe we even felt our actions were justified.

> **We must listen with intent and speak with purpose.**

When we are serious about living out our faith, our lives will become different. God changes our hearts. In turn, our minds are changed to think after the ways of Him (Romans 12:2). While He does not command us to never feel anger or be opinionated, God does make clear that we should slow down our response, meaning we must control how we respond. We must listen with intent and speak with purpose. When we trust God to be in control, we can learn to control our anger and better manage our tongue. We will be better positioned to reject ungodly behavior and be more willing to be obedient to Him and His Word. We will accept our responsibility to be quick, be slow, get rid of, and humbly accept all that God requires us to do. This is our call to action. As we strive to live a life pleasing to God, we should compare our ways to His ways. The way we do this is to hold ourselves up to the Word God planted in our hearts when we accepted Him and He granted us salvation. For it is how we live out God's Word in our lives that reflects our level of faith in Him. Living out His Word is what will save our souls.

Father, we know that our behavior is not always acceptable to You. We don't always behave with the intent and purpose of living in Your image. We ask that You teach us how to be more like You in our interactions with others. We pray to be better listeners and doers of Your Word. Let us not be quick to anger but be more aware of how to be in control. In Jesus's name, Amen.

Day 3

Banner of Love

Pure and genuine religion in the sight of God the Father means caring for orphans and widows in their distress and refusing to let the world corrupt you. — James 1:27 (NLT)

Leaving my appointment, I was stopped behind two elderly women. The Holy Spirit spoke to me: *give her money*. I questioned this. I knew without a doubt I did not have any cash. My spirit became chaotic as I stood there trying to find a reason for this conviction. Reluctantly, I looked in my purse. I took out money. I counted it. It was the exact amount the Holy Spirit had convicted me of. Walking away from the women, I heard one say to the other, "You were worried we could not make it home; God always makes a way."

He uses each of us to be a help to others.

As believers, we should never consider whether God will use us, because He will (2 Timothy 2:21). We must be concerned to not miss His call to be used. If our faith does not convict us to be examples of Christ's character and love, we must examine ourselves. When we have God-given faith, we express joy for our salvation through acts of service and obedience. We are prone to show sacrificial love as we enter the suffering of others. As believers we should have a heart for society's most vulnerable people, people who cannot provide for themselves but rely on the benevolence of others, including strangers, for their basic needs. We are called to treat others with empathy and compassion. Caring for others who could never give back to you is some of what God requires. Showing sacrificial love is what Christ did for us. Is it a surprise that He would call us to do the same? His willingness to endure suffering for our sake is the ultimate display of love and compassion. Each day we should strive to be aware of opportunities where we can be an example of Christ's love to the world. Just like those two women who trusted Him to provide for them, I know He uses each of us to be a help to others. We must be ready to as He says to move.

Father, we thank You for the ability and desire to care for others. We confess that at times we get discouraged, but we pray to always be available to be used by You. Keep our minds and hearts open to helping those in need so the world may see and know that it is You who work through us. In Jesus's name, Amen.

As believers our focus should be to live a life that honors Christ.

Day 4

Perfect Love

Yes, indeed, it is good when you obey the royal law as found in the Scriptures: "Love your neighbor as yourself." But if you favor some people over others, you are committing a sin. You are guilty of breaking the law. — James 2:8–9 (NLT)

Have you watched the news lately? It's filled with stories of crime, government infighting, and war. If I did not know any better, I'd think we are incapable of living with love and compassion in today's world. Imagine the peace we all would experience if we loved ourselves as Christ loves us and we extended that love to one another. This is part of what we are purposed to do. God has called us to reflect His love to one another. When we put ourselves in our neighbors' shoes, love comes to life in our situations. When we apply grace to our own lives, we condition ourselves to live a life of gratitude. Our gratitude compels us to give freely to those around us, for we accept the fact that every good thing we have belongs to God. As believers we should reflect this in all we do.

> **Every good thing we have belongs to God.**

When we act in the best interest of our neighbors, we fulfill God's law (Matthew 22:35–40). And favoritism, no matter how we address it, goes against who God is. God never looks upon anyone more highly than another. We are all the same to Him, and He is merciful to us all. He even calls for us to love our enemies (Matthew 5:43–45). How many times have we read or heard this and thought, *Really, God? I don't know if I can do that.* Christ proved when He walked upon the earth that perfect love exists when He asked God to forgive His enemies even as He hung dying on the Cross (Luke 23:34). How difficult is it to forgive those who come against us? This level of love cannot exist without Christ at the center of our lives. We must reject self-serving thoughts about what we can gain from others. We must not look down on our neighbors or think highly of ourselves. We must examine our actions and thoughts, confess our sins, and address our own acts of favoritism. Love our neighbors in words and deeds. Share the good news of salvation with others. Keep the interests of our neighbors at the center of what we do. Keeping Christ as our central focus serves as the guiding light and example of selflessness to live out His calling on our lives.

Father, help us be generous to others without hesitation. Let us tend freely to one another's needs so others may see Your goodness and love in our actions. We ask to not feel weary in our well-doing. Let us be mindful that to show favoritism is a sin. Give us the spirit of loving everyone equally. In Jesus's name, Amen.

Day 5

God Know Best

For the person who keeps all of the laws except one is as guilty as a person who has broken all of God's laws. James 2:10 (NLT)

We had arrived as a family at the hospital on the day of our daughter's tonsillectomy. All checked in, prepped, and wheeled into the operating room, she tried her best to change our minds on her having surgery. She even stated she had to use the restroom. My 'mom reaction' prompted me to tell her to lie down and take a quick sniff of laughing gas then I would take her to the restroom. Well, that wasn't the truth. She sniffed and was asleep for her surgery. In the waiting room I can remember feeling terrible that I had lied to my child. And everyone in that room heard me speak about it off and on until I was able to see our daughter in the recovery room. Why did I feel so bad about lying to our daughter? After all, it was for a good reason. It was

> **To follow our own judgement and disobey God's laws only separates us from him.**

the only way I could get her to cooperate in order get her needs met.

I often wondered how a simple sin could carry so much weight. God gives us spiritual direction on how to live in the best way when He gave us His laws. As believers we cannot not pick and choose which parts to follow. When we fail to apply His laws to our lives we live outside of His purpose for us. We willingly invite sin into our lives and our disobedience becomes an act of questioning His authority. *How can we proclaim to believe in God and choose not to obey His word?* God knows what is best for us. Yet, the harsh reality is each of us is guilty of disobeying His laws (Rom 3:23). Our disobedience can be seen as a projection of us knowing better than God in our situations. To follow our own judgement separates us from Him. Eve reflected this when she allowed her own judgement to outweigh God's Word by knowingly eating the forbidden fruit (Gen 3:6). While Jesus intercedes on our behalf we must live in obedience to His Word. They are our guide to living holy and pleasing unto Him.

Father, I come before you acknowledging my sins. I ask your forgiveness Please remove anything that separates me from You and Your purpose for my life. I pray You give me the discipline to live according to Your Word so I may live eternally in Your kingdom. Thank you for being a merciful Savior. In Jesus' name, Amen

Day 6

Faith Works

What good is it, dear brothers and sisters, if you say you have faith but don't show it by your actions? Can that kind of faith save anyone?
— James 2:14 (NLT)

> True faith moves us to portray the character of Christ.

We laughed. We ate. We talked about everything that had happened in our lives since we'd last caught up. The server brought out a meal ordered for takeaway. We gathered our things and left. Upon exiting the restaurant, my friend placed the hot meal in the hands of a homeless man seated on the sidewalk. His smile reflected how grateful he was. "Why did you do that?" someone asked. *Isn't this what faith does? It causes us to move in a Christlike manner.*

True faith changes our hearts. Brings us into relationship with Christ. Compels us into action. Causes us to live out our faith through good deeds out of obedience to God, which is our duty (Luke 17:10). This is what God-given faith looks like. It is faith that works to be an example of Christ. It is faith that moves us to portray the character of God. To serve the poor. To feed the hungry. To fight oppression. To love our neighbors. These are some of the ways we answer God's call to having true faith. However, professing our faith alone is not enough. What benefit is there to say "I have faith in God" yet do nothing to live out this belief? Would it have benefited anyone had my friend only prayed that God bless the homeless man as she walked by? While prayer is necessary, so are good deeds. My friend's show of Christlike love resulted in meeting the need of providing a meal for the homeless man. Our actions should model Christ. This helps others, especially nonbelievers, to see Him in this world. Good deeds prove our profession of faith is sincere. A profession of faith followed by a change in our thoughts and behavior of good works confirms our salvation and belief in God (2 Peter 1:5–11). In turn, our actions of godly love can draw others to Christ.

Father, bless me to be a person of faith in action. I want to be used by You to be an example of Christ's character in the world. I surrender all my talents, resources, and life to You. Teach me how to live out my true faith in You so I may be a blessing to others. In Jesus's name, Amen.

To follow our own judgment separates us from God.

Day 7

Power of the Tongue

Indeed, we all make many mistakes. For if we could control our tongues, we would be perfect and could also control ourselves in every other way. — James 3:2 (NLT)

Complaining and murmuring work in contrast to our faith.

I went through a season where I would sing a song of praise when I felt frustration setting in. I spoke. I sang. To myself. To my situation. To God. This calmed me. It brought my focus to Him. It made me pause. My initial emotions would subside. I was better postured to invite God into my moment of frustration. I would gain mental space to choose my words better. My focus and attitude would change for the better. I was in control of my response for that moment. Or perhaps I was better equipped because my focus was on inviting Christ into the moment.

Words are powerful. They can build up or bring down people. They can uplift or bring chaos into our lives. Our tongue is so powerful that we alone cannot control it. We need God's help. Maybe, just maybe, if we directed our minds to giving thanks in the midst of our frustration, we would better manage our words and actions. We must practice speaking words that give life, hope, and encouragement, for when our tongue is harnessed by God, we uplift our situations. When we speak life unto ourselves and others, we reflect the character of God. Complaining and murmuring work in contrast to our faith. They are to the devil what praise is to God, as they reveal our unbelief in God to be in control. Jesus taught that our words are revelations of what is in our hearts (Matthew 12:34-37). How can we claim faith in God yet complain, revealing our disbelief in His authority? We cannot. We should not give power to our old nature of unbelief but rely on Christ to continue to change our hearts and, in turn, our speech. We must resist stumbling back to our old heart from before we accepted Christ. We must be committed in our walk with Him. Trust Him to continue to renew our minds (Romans 12:2). Stand firm knowing that the One who blessed us with God-given faith has already turned our hearts to Him. He can also turn our speech to what is pure and true. We must trust Him to do so.

Father, we thank You for changing our hearts. We ask that our words and tones would be reflections of You. Let us not be a hindrance to Your blessings in our lives. Let our words uplift others and bring glory to You at all times. In Jesus's name, Amen.

Day 8

Value of Wisdom

For jealousy and selfishness are not God's kind of wisdom. Such things are earthly, unspiritual, and demonic. For wherever there is jealousy and selfish ambition, there you will find disorder and evil of every kind. — James 3:15–16 (NLT)

We can identify the source of our wisdom based on our speech and actions.

Our speech and actions reveal the wisdom we adhere to: true wisdom or earthly wisdom. True wisdom derives from God. It reveals itself through meekness, humility, peace, and selflessness. True wisdom produces good fruits, as it aims to reflect the character of Christ. Earthly wisdom is not derived from God. It reveals itself through selfish ambition, jealousy, evilness, and confusion. Such wisdom could never please God. Its focus is earthly pleasures, and it has no connection to God-given faith. Earthly wisdom does not and cannot help us beyond this physical world. Its fruit is limited to what we can accumulate here on earth.

True wisdom begins with trust in God's sovereignty. We must abandon our human logic, acknowledge our sinful nature, and accept that only God is perfect. It is according to His will, not according to our desires, that He provides for us. When God's way for our lives reveals itself to be different than our desires, we must be obedient in accepting His plan for our lives. We must be led by His plan even if we disagree or do not understand (Proverbs 3:5-8). We must let go of selfish ambition and jealousy. They rob of us of our identity in Christ and prevent us from trusting Him. Relying on earthly wisdom makes it hard for us to accept Spirit-led correction, causing us to turn inward and increase our reliance on self. These things go against God and bring His judgment upon us (Deuteronomy 4:24). We must live for God's glory as we pray to reap the harvest of eternal life. We must resist the temptation of self-reliance and seek to follow true wisdom.

Father, we thank You for the help of the Holy Spirit. We pray for discernment to know what is from You and what is Your will for our lives. We pray for discipline to obey and accept all that You have planned for us. Correct us and convict us so we may be a living example of what is good and true. In Jesus's name, Amen.

Day 9

A Friend of God

You adulterers! Don't you realize that friendship with the world makes you an enemy of God? I say it again: If you want to be a friend of the world, you make yourself an enemy of God.
— James 4:4 (NLT)

> As long as we are consumed with the ways of the world, we will remain in a state of spiritual turmoil.

Can we love Jesus and continue to be consumed with the ways of the world? We cannot (Romans 6:1–6). Believers who continue to live according to worldly wisdom are not living as friends of God. We reject God's ways when we stay in active pursuit of earthly wisdom and rewards. Being in friendship with the world is to love the ways of sin. It is never living in complete cooperation with the Holy Spirit but denying Christ's transformative power full access in our lives. We all struggle with old habits of sin, as our spirit and flesh are constantly at war with one another. Yet we do not fully accept the perfect love of God. Why is this? Could it be that we are not content in our relationship with God?

We should reject behaviors that go against God's laws, for such behaviors are self-serving and end in judgment. As long as we are consumed with the ways of the world, we will remain in a state of confusion and spiritual turmoil. We will remain separated from God. However, when Christ is at the center of our lives, our hearts remain focused on Him. We become content with our own journey. We want the things He wants for us. We can make requests of God, knowing that our motives and hearts are without guilt. We accept when His plan differs from our desires. As believers we must submit ourselves to God and stand firm during our tests of faith. Resist doing evil. And draw close to God. When we honestly examine ourselves, we can identify our sinful ways and petition God for forgiveness and discipline to stay in His will. Such behavior shows that we are a friend of God.

Father, we thank You that we are in relationship with You. We petition You for the Holy Spirit to always guide us to what's good and pure and true so we may continue to grow our faith in You. Bless us that we may not be overtaken by the cares of this world but stay committed in our relationship with You. In Jesus's name, Amen.

Earthly wisdom separates us from God.

Godly wisdom causes us to accept His plans for our lives.

Day 10

He Holds Our Tomorrows

How do you know what your life will be like tomorrow? Your life is like the morning fog—it's here a little while, then it's gone. What you ought to say is, "If the Lord wants us to, we will live and do this or that." — James 4:14–15 (NLT)

If it's the Lord's will. That was the ending we kids said when we spoke of the future. As adults we continue to speak the same way to our parents. They will not accept anything less. It's because they know that which they instilled in us. Humans control nothing, not even ourselves. It is only by God's mercy we can accomplish anything. We are foolish to think we have the power to do anything on our own or to know what our future will be. Godly wisdom teaches that nothing we do is of our own strength. Earthly wisdom teaches that we are in control and capable of making things happen on our own. Looking inward brings about expectations of what our outcome should be and causes us to look less to God. This brings about pride and self-reliance. This way of being is not godly.

We must not let selfish ambition rule over our lives.

Planning and preparation are not sinful acts. It is our failure to acknowledge our dependence on God in the plans we put together that makes us arrogant and boastful and ultimately sinful. We must never forget that only God can allow our plans to happen (Proverbs 16:9). Good or evil, God can use our acts for His purpose. Accordingly, we must learn to accept God's outcomes, especially when they are not what we envision. The division of true and earthly wisdom sets the tone for our responses during our disappointments. Earthly wisdom will make us feel resentful and angry and bitter. It will separate us from God and cause us to look within ourselves. Godly wisdom causes us to accept our outcomes no matter what they are, for we know we are subject to God's perfect plan. We must not let selfish ambition rule over our lives. Seek to follow godly wisdom. It will ensure God's blessings upon our lives (1 John 3:22).

Father, forgive us when we boast of our tomorrow. We know that only You hold our next second, our next minute, our entire future. Let us seek Your plans for our lives and not those of our own ambition. Bless us with godly wisdom so our words and actions will be acceptable to You. In Jesus's name, Amen.

Day 11

Much to Do

Remember, it is sin to know what you ought to do and then not to do it. — James 4:17 (NLT)

> **He has given us a helper in the Holy Spirit.**

Have you ever felt conflicted between what you wanted to do and what you knew to be the right thing to do? Maybe you have wrestled with doing what was right when you truly wanted to do the opposite. Did a voice inside you convince you to do what you knew to be the right thing? Knowing God's ways is not enough to ensure our His blessings upon our lives. We must apply that knowledge in our lives. When we fail to do what we know is right, we sin, and we dishonor Him (Psalms 86:11). When we study the Scriptures and keep His Word in our hearts, we are better equipped to stand against temptations and endure our tests of faith. We build ourselves up mentally and spiritually, and we better resist returning to our sinful ways. We must actively participate in our relationship with Christ, as it is not good enough for us to just avoid evil. When we sit by passively and let evil happen, we are no less sinful than the one who willfully commits the act (Luke 12:47).

As believers our focus should be to live a life that honors Christ. He has promised we have all we need to do so (1 Corinthians 10:13). We cannot continue to live in sin and expect to live in eternity with God or experience His fullness in our lives. Whether it is through our actions, words, or thoughts, we must resist what does not honor Him. We will not always get it right. At times we may stumble back into our old sinful ways. But we should confess our sins and correct our ways so we may grow in our relationship with Christ. He has given us a helper in the Holy Spirit (Romans 8:26). It is the indwelling of the Spirit who speaks to us of the right way to go. We must obey it. There is no situation He cannot deliver us from, as He promised His strength is greater than our fears and weaknesses (Deuteronomy 31:6). We have His Word to guide us on how we should abide in Him. It gives us instructions on how to walk in true faith. We must always be willing to live our lives faithfully, commit our hearts to Him, and find strength in His promises.

Father, bless us to have a heart that always seeks to serve and please you. Convict us to live in Your will. Keep our hearts and minds focused on You so we may experience the fullness of all you have purposed for our lives. In Jesus's name, Amen.

Day 12

Good Stewardship

Look here, you rich people: Weep and groan with anguish because of all the terrible troubles ahead of you. — James 5:1 (NLT)

> God does not call for the wealthy to not be rich.

There are many wealthy Christians in the Bible. Isaac (Genesis 26:12–14), King David (1 Chronicles 29:28), and Lydia (Acts 16:14–21) are a few. Isaac did not hoard the wealth he inherited. He used it to bless many nations. David restored Saul's land to his grandson Mephibosheth (2 Samuel 9:7). Lydia risked her business and reputation when she invited and received Paul and Silas into her home. These wealthy believers were people who trusted in God, not in their riches or status. Their hearts were devoted to God, and they honored Him with their resources. They understood the requirements and accepted the responsibilities of being a good manager over all that God entrusted to them. And God blessed their riches for generations.

God does not call for the wealthy to not be rich. He simply requires proper use of everything we have at our disposal. It has been shown that through the love of money we invite evil into our lives (1 Timothy 6:9-10). When we pursue accumulation of wealth here on earth, we subject ourselves to the possibility of traps of self-ambition, greed, idolatry, stealing from the poor, and hoarding our resources. These behaviors are sinful and will work against us. The Bible calls for us not to hoard our resources but to share out of abundance as an example of Christ's love. After all it is not riches that are good or evil. It is our sinful nature. How we fit our wealth and resources into our relationship with Christ determines whether they are good or evil. As believers, followers of Christ, and a group of believers, the church, we must bring glory to God through proper use of our money, time, and talents.

Father, we are thankful for the opportunities to use our resources to be an example of Your love to others. We pray to always have a mind and heart to use our money, time, and talents to honor You in everything we do. Let us not be removed from You because we lust after what we do not have. In Jesus's name, Amen.

Do not
be moved
by
fear or pressure.
Trust God
to
fulfill all
He has promised.

Day 13

The Blessing in Waiting

Dear brothers and sisters, be patient as you wait for the Lord's return. Consider the farmers who patiently wait for the rains in the fall and in the spring. They eagerly look for the valuable harvest to ripen. You, too, must be patient. Take courage, for the coming of the Lord is near.
— James 5:7–8 (NLT)

There are times when we must wait on God. When we seek God, we are able to look to Him with an expectation of an end to our prayers. Just like the farmer, we must not sit idly awaiting Christ's return. We must accept our responsibilities and faithfully carry out the work God has called us to do. We must do so with patience, as this provides the foundation believers need to rely on God unconditionally. This gives us strength to endure the difficult times in our lives as we trust God for provision. Honoring His sovereignty allows us to trust in Him

> We must not give in to our human limits for God has promised to bless those who wait on Him.

and His promises no matter what hardships we face. Do not be moved by fear or pressure or selfish ambition. Trust God to fulfill all He has promised.

There are plenty of believers in the Bible who waited patiently on God and were rewarded. Job (Job 42:10–16), David (2 Samuel 5:4–5), and Hannah (1 Samuel 1:27–28) were a few. Their waits on God reflected purpose in waiting and proved that God hears and answers the prayers of the faithful-hearted. As believers we must continue to grow our faith by learning to wait on God. Only He can give us the strength to continue our walk with Him, even when we become discouraged and tempted. We must not give in to our human limits, for God has promised to bless those who wait on Him (Isaiah 30:18). We must never curse our waiting season but use it for our good and God's glory. Wait with purpose and intention. Continually pursue God's heart. Use your wait to draw closer to God, as waiting on Him strengthens your faith. Look to Him for His perfect timing, for we do not know when the Lord will return. We do know He will fulfill His promise to come again. Stay faithful and committed in your relationship with Him so you may live a life pleasing to Him.

Father, we thank You for Your faithfulness. We ask for strength to stand firm in our faith during our trials and temptations. We know in our hearts that You will keep Your promise to return and make things right. During our wait, we ask You to draw near to us. Just as You rewarded Job, David, and Hannah, we look for Your blessings upon our lives. In Jesus's name, Amen.

Day 14

Prone to Wander

My brothers, if anyone among you wanders from the truth and someone brings him back, let him know that whoever brings back a sinner from his wandering will save his soul from death and will cover a multitude of sins. — James 5:19–20 (NLT)

> Believers must attempt to bring back the spiritually weak who wander from God.

I enjoy being in nature. Long walks in the woods and hikes up mountains bring me peace and an intense connection to God. I always map my route prior to heading out. It's nothing for me to extend my walks and put away my map. I do this as a way to be fully present in the beauty and peace of nature. One time I was enjoying myself so much that I ventured past my turnaround point. I had left the trail. Immersed in nature's beauty, I was unaware of how far and in which direction I had walked. I was lost. I had strayed from the path.

In the same way, we can get lost in our walk with God. Distractions and demands in life can overtake us and create distance in our relationship with Him. We know the way we are to go. We know the character of the One we are to emulate. Yet we sometimes lose sight of these things, and we wander away from the truth. We wander away from God. Living in God's truth should be our focus. As believers we accept this responsibility not only for ourselves but for each other. The importance of community reflected in verses 19–20 is best illustrated in Ecclesiastes 4:9–12, which states that two people are better off than one, for they can help each other succeed; if one person falls, the other can reach out and help. This togetherness and community are essential to our spiritual growth and maturity as believers. It provides a space to focus on meeting the needs of others as well as our own.

So what happens when a believer leaves community and strays from God? The community must act. The Christlike love of believers makes room for genuine care for others. Believers must attempt to bring back the spiritually weak who wander from God. James doesn't tell us how, only that an earnest attempt must be made to bring back to Christ those who stray. This is not a light responsibility. Its benefits are great: a soul will be saved from death. We all stray at one time or another. We are blessed to have community. We are fortunate for community that chases us when we ourselves wander from the loving arms of our Father.

Father, we pray to always be spiritually strong. For the times we do wander from Your presence, we ask to never be out of sight from community and their willingness to help us restore ourselves to You. We thank you for its gift of togetherness. May we always seek to be a part of it. In Jesus's name, Amen.

ABOUT THE FOREWORD AUTHOR

Dr. Zelphine Smith-Dixon has a long-standing history in improving achievement for students. She was the Georgia State Special Education Director and served as the Board President for the National Association of State Directors of Special Education (NASDSE). She is the Rockdale County Chief Student Support Officer.

Dr. Smith-Dixon lives in Conyers, Georgia, with her husband, Marki Dixon, and three kids, Myles, Megan, and Mason. She submits to the vision of her lead pastor, Bishop William H. Murphy, III, and serves as the Director of the Ministerial Alliance at the dReam Center Church of Atlanta.

She leads largely in the community as the educational development chair for the Covington area alumnae chapter of Delta Sigma Theta Sorority, Inc.

Her heart to serve is unmatched, and her willingness to lead in excellence is a trendsetter!

ABOUT THE AUTHOR

Runettia Guess is a passionate Christian, resilient and faithful through life's trials. Overcoming the unimaginable loss of her son has strengthened her faith and inspired her to motivate others. She serves as a certified mental health coach and motivational speaker.

Runettia lives in Jacksonville, Florida, with her daughter, Jessica.

Milton Keynes UK
Ingram Content Group UK Ltd.
UKHW020341031224
451863UK00013B/642